Dear Brig......y

Sorry this has taken so
long to get to ya. I hope
you enjoy it! Come and see
us soon!
                                — Sarah

A Gospel of a Different Color

Exploring the Gospel of John

Frank Drenner

WESTBOW
PRESS®
A DIVISION OF THOMAS NELSON
& ZONDERVAN

Unless otherwise noted, all scripture quotations are
from the New Revised Standard Version Bible, copyright
© 1989, Division of Christian Education of the National
Council of the Churches of Christ in the United States
of America. Used by permission. All rights reserved.

WestBow Press books may be ordered through
booksellers or by contacting:

WestBow Press
A Division of Thomas Nelson & Zondervan
1663 Liberty Drive
Bloomington, IN 47403
www.westbowpress.com
1 (866) 928-1240

ISBN: 978-1-5127-4079-0 (sc)
ISBN: 978-1-5127-4081-3 (hc)
ISBN: 978-1-5127-4080-6 (e)

Library of Congress Control Number: 2016907445

Print information available on the last page.

WestBow Press rev. date: 05/04/2016

Contents

Introduction

In Honor of My Grandfather, Donald Guffey

When I went to seminary twenty years ago, I took with me very little knowledge of the Bible. Although I grew up in the church, I did not have the same level of Bible knowledge as my seminary friends. This fact had both advantages and disadvantages. My advantage was that when a professor mentioned a controversial idea, I had little previous understanding to defend. I was free to learn and develop in the seminary; this latitude made those years that much more special. On the other hand, my lack of knowledge led to some embarrassing moments, like when we had a practicum class during the New Testament section of the first-year Bible survey course. We had finished the Synoptic Gospels—Matthew, Mark, and Luke— so called because their content is similar. Now in John, I demonstrated my ignorance by asking, "Is it really so different?"

Well, yeah! (It always helps to read before speaking.)

My grandfather, who is ninety-four, has lots of sayings he'll throw out in conversation every now and then. When my cousin Ron and I would play spades at Mema and Papaw's house, someone would play a surprising card, and he would exclaim, "That's a horse of a different color!"

Well, when I first became familiar with the fourth gospel, I found myself thinking often of Papaw. Something unexplained or surprising—not found in the more well-known gospels—would happen, and I would hear his voice in my head saying, "That's a horse of a different color!" John became the "gospel of a different color" for me. As I studied and taught John over the years, the idea began to grow of compiling into a book the insights I have learned and shared. So it is only fitting for me to dedicate the book to Papaw. He is a man of great faith and has taught me much about life—just by watching how he lives his own. Thank you, Papaw. I love you.

Each section of this book includes reflection questions for the preacher and teacher. Good preaching is built upon relationships with the congregation members and a sense of shared community. Great Bible teaching is grounded in humility and an interest in further growth through study. The questions will aid in the development of sermons and lessons, with an eye toward life application. At the end of each chapter is a sermon I preached at Custer Road United Methodist Church in Plano, Texas, where I served as senior associate pastor while writing this book. The sermons match the themes offered in each chapter.

I am very grateful to the good folk at Custer Road who helped shape this book by participating in Bible studies and Sunday school series I offered during my ministry there.

Peace and Joy,

Pastor Frank

Custer Road United Methodist Church

January 2015 - May 2016

CHAPTER 1

Do You Believe This?

I have always been an avid sports fan, particularly of baseball and football. Growing up in the 1970s, I remember very clearly seeing fan-made signs posted at nearly every televised game. They simply read *John 3:16* (I rarely see them today). I never knew what that meant. Broadcasters didn't try to explain it. Since the sign was visible at nearly every sporting event, it was not tied to an individual team or a particular sport. What did the name John, followed by a number 3, a colon, and the number 16 mean? It was only much later that I realized it was a Scripture reference. So I pulled out the third-grade Bible presented to me in 1979 by my home church, First United Methodist Church of Bay City, Texas. I found John. I found chapter 3. I found verse 16. And I read this very familiar verse:

> For God so loved the world that he gave his only begotten son, that whoever believes in him may not perish but have eternal life. (Revised Standard Version)

Years later, I heard this particular verse referenced as "the Bible within the Bible." In other words, if you memorized only one verse of the whole Bible, this should be the one. It contains all you need to know.

Right there, near the middle of the sentence is the word "believes." "Whoever believes." That's every one of us. If we believe, we have eternal life. It's Jesus's mission statement in an easy-to-remember form. I do not know how many times I have participated in churches that are creating, learning, or rewriting a mission statement. None has ever been so clearly and directly stated. But for Jesus, this was not something to hang on a wall or publish in a bulletin or on a website; it was a way of life. It was an invitation for others to a new life. Here are some quick references to *believe, believes,* and *believed* in John. You're welcome to pull out your Bible concordance to discover every single reference.

- At the end of the miracle at Cana story: "his disciples believed in him" (2:11).
- The disciples remember the temple cleansing following Jesus's resurrection: "they believed the scripture and the word that Jesus had spoken" (2:22).
- "When [Jesus] was in Jerusalem many believed in his name because of the signs that he was doing" (2:23).
- Jesus said, "Whoever believes in the Son has eternal life" (3:36).
- After Jesus spends a few days in a Samaritan village: "And many more believed because of his word" (4:41).
- A man whose son fell ill: "Jesus said to him, 'Unless you see signs and wonders you will not believe.' The official said to him, 'Sir, come down before my little boy dies.' Jesus said to him, 'Go; your son will live.' The man believed the word that Jesus spoke to him and went on his way. As he was going down his slaves met him and told him that his child was alive. So he asked them the hour when he began to recover, and they said to him, 'Yesterday at one in the afternoon the fever left him.' The father realized this was the hour when Jesus said to him, 'Your son will live.' So he himself believed,

along with his whole household" (John 4:46–54). Three references in one brief story!

The word "believe" occurs 173 times in the Bible. The word "believed" occurs an additional sixty-seven times. But notice how the Gospel of John dominates the use of the word. Of the 173 times "believe" is found in the Bible, an astounding fifty-seven of them are included in John. Likewise, of the sixty-seven "believed" references, twenty-four are found in John. Obviously, John has an exaggerated interest in the word. But why? As we explore this gospel of a different color, we will focus on certain stories as they relate to Jesus's core mission: to bring folks to him. We will not interpret every verse of the gospel, but several speak directly to this mission.

A Man Born Blind (9:1–41)

Jesus's healing ministry was powerful, transforming many lives from brokenness to wholeness. A great example is the healing in chapter 9 of a young man who was born blind. But this is no ordinary healing story. It is filled with invitations to believe in Jesus, some of which are accepted and others rejected. The disciples ask Jesus, "Rabbi, who sinned, this man or the parents, that he was born blind?"

"Neither this man nor his parents sinned," Jesus answers. "He was born blind so that God's works might be revealed in him" (9:3). Jesus heals the man and tells him to go and wash at the pool of Siloam, which he did.

Upon his washing he begins to see, and folk notice: "Is this not the man who used to sit and beg?" (9:8). He says yes, that he has been healed. Unable to understand the situation, they take the man to the religious authorities for an explanation.

The religious leaders immediately distrust the man, and when he explains that his sight was gained by the work of Jesus, their response is acute: "This man [Jesus] is not from God, for he does not observe the sabbath" (9:16). Others, perhaps even Nicodemus, whom we will hear more from in chapters 3 and 19, dispute the accusation by asking, "How can a man who is a sinner perform such signs?" (9:18). "The Jews did not believe that he had been blind and had received his sight until they called the parents of the man." His parents confirm that this is in fact their son, who was blind, but out of fear of being put out of the synagogue, they will not name Jesus as the source of his healing (9:22).

The leaders call for the man again and question him once more. He is adamant that Jesus healed him. Defiantly, he says, "Do you also want to become his disciples?" (9:27), and they respond by throwing the man out of the synagogue.

Later, Jesus seeks out the man and asks, "Do you believe in the Son of Man?" (9:35).

"And who is he, sir? Tell me, that I may believe in him."

Jesus said, "You have seen him, and the one speaking to you is he."

"[The man] said, 'Lord, I believe.' And he worshipped him" (10:38).

For the Preacher and Teacher

This story contrasts the faith of one born unable to see with the spiritual blindness of the religious leaders. This is at the heart of Jesus's mission: to find, save, and heal the lost. In his day, those afflicted with unexplainable or incurable conditions were understood as either cursed by God or the result of another's sin. Jesus transforms those the world would reject with his invitation to a new life.

Our ability to see is not determined by the function of our eyes but our faith. As the man's parents say, "Ask him; he is of age. He will speak for himself" (9:21).

When did you first believe? Is your belief the result of Jesus's invitation? How did you hear those words, and how did you respond? What keeps people from hearing Jesus's invitation? What pressures might they feel before saying yes? How does John's prolific use of the word "believe" affect your understanding of Jesus's ministry?

A Sermon

This sermon was preached following the Epiphany, a time to consider different manifestations of God in our lives. The identity of Jesus is revealed to the disciples in the sign at the wedding. After professing their belief in Jesus, they begin their ministry.

A Wedding Like No Other: From
Belief to Discipleship
John 2:1–11
January 17, 2016
Custer Road United Methodist Church
Lectio Teaching Worship Service

Over the years, I have presided at many weddings. For an outside observer, a wedding is sometimes funny, sometimes boring, and sometimes beautiful. For the preacher, weddings offer a unique level of stress. I have never participated in an uneventful wedding.

One time, the groom had his father as his best man. Just as the couple was about to say their vows to each other at the climax of the service, Dad grinned at his son to reveal that he was wearing vampire teeth.

Thanks, Dad.

Another time, I was co-officiating a wedding with a minister of another denomination—the bride's pastor when she was young. I invited the visiting pastor to offer the homily, since he knew the couple personally. His message was long, about as long as the entire service on its own. Then he offered them a wedding gift. Just as he mentioned the gift, someone brought a potted tree into the sanctuary and left it in the side aisle. A tree. As a wedding gift.

Thanks, Pastor.

Or there was the time when the sound systems of the church and a hotel across the street somehow synched right during the Lord's Prayer. The Lord's Prayer is not printed in the wedding liturgy; it must be prayed from memory. So it was very frustrating to hear the DJ at the reception at the hotel introduce the next song just as I was leading the congregation in prayer at the church. I have not concentrated so hard on the prayer before or since!

Thanks, Mr. DJ.

I don't know if the wedding Jesus and his mother attended in Cana was crazy like that or not, but the reception was certainly memorable. After the party has gone on for some time, the chief steward learns that the wine supply has run out. Mary overhears the concern and brings it to Jesus's attention. Jesus says, "Woman, what concern is that to you and to me? My hour has not yet come" (2:4). Have you ever referred to your mother as "woman"? You might—*once*.

Unbothered, Mary turns to the steward and says, "Do whatever he tells you" (2:5). And, of course, Jesus acts as his mother anticipated. Seeing six giant stone water jars, he orders them filled with water. These jars could have held up to thirty gallons each.

After each jar is filled, the stewards bring out some of the water, now transformed into wine, and give the chief steward a taste. Shocked at the quality of the wine, he says to the groom something like, "Listen, buddy, the normal way to do it is to serve the expensive stuff first; then after everyone is hammered, you roll out the cheap stuff. By then no one can tell the difference! But you've saved the good stuff until now!"

The gospel writer refers to this act as a sign. A sign is an extraordinary act in the midst of an ordinary occasion. What's more ordinary than a wedding reception? Another sign happens later in chapter 6 when Jesus transforms a kid's lunch into enough food to feed thousands and still has twelve baskets of leftovers. We see a sign and then reflect on the goodness and power of God.

In a gospel largely absent of parables, the wedding of Cana serves as a parable of God's abundant grace. Jesus, without any explicit request—and certainly no one at the reception does anything to deserve the overflowing grace—brings nearly 200 gallons of excellent wine. John tells us the disciples see this sign and "believe in him." Immediately preceding this story, at the end of chapter 1, John narrates the calling of the disciples. Jesus calls Philip, and Philip invites Nathanael with the words, "We have found the one Moses wrote about in the Law ... Jesus, Joseph's son, of Nazareth" (1:45). Nathanael infamously responds, "Can anything good come out of Nazareth?" and Philip says, "Come and see." At the wedding, the disciples see Jesus as he truly is "and his disciples believed in him" (2:11).

The book of Isaiah is one of the most complicated of the Old Testament. Written over many years, Isaiah speaks of the destruction of Jerusalem in 587 BCE, the enslavement of the Israelites to Babylon, and of the hope of their eventual restoration. After four generations, the people returned to Jerusalem and resettled Judah. Chapter 62 speaks a word of hope and transformation for a long-suffering people:

> For Zion's sake I will not keep silent, and for Jerusalem's sake I will not rest, until her vindication shines out like the dawn, and her salvation like a burning torch. The nations shall see your vindication, and all the kings your glory; and you shall be called by a new name that the mouth of the LORD will give. You shall be a crown of beauty in the hand of the LORD, and a royal diadem in the hand of your God. You shall no more be termed Forsaken, and your land shall no more be termed Desolate; but you shall be called My Delight Is In Her, and your land Married; for the LORD delights in you, and your land shall be married. For as a young man marries a young woman, so shall your builder marry you, and as the bridegroom rejoices over the bride, so shall your God rejoice over you. (Isaiah 62:1–5)

God promises to restore the people: their grief, their brokenness, their homes, and their very identity.

They will be given a new name—no longer referred to as *forsaken,* the land no longer called *desolate.* Instead, the people will be crowned with a royal diadem, a gift of God's glory. As Jesus performed his first sign at a wedding, so God speaks of the common Old Testament metaphor of groom/bride to describe God's relationship to Israel. God will rejoice in the restored community.

Throughout his epistles, the apostle Paul challenged the churches to live out their faith by exercising their spiritual gifts:

> Now concerning spiritual gifts, brothers and sisters, I do not want you to be uninformed. You know that when you were pagans, you were enticed and led astray to idols that could not speak. Therefore I want you to understand that no one speaking by the Spirit of God ever says 'Let Jesus be cursed!' and no one can say 'Jesus is Lord' except by the Holy Spirit. Now there are varieties of gifts, but the same Spirit; and there are varieties of services, but the same Lord; and there are varieties of activities, but it is the same God who activates all of them in everyone.To each is given

the manifestation of the Spirit for the common good.To one is given through the Spirit the utterance of wisdom, and to another the utterance of knowledge according to the same Spirit, to another faith by the same Spirit, to another gifts of healing by the one Spirit, to another the working of miracles, to another prophecy, to another the discernment of spirits, to another various kinds of tongues, to another the interpretation of tongues. All these are activated by one and the same Spirit, who allots to each one individually just as the Spirit chooses. (1 Corinthians 12:1–11)

The Israelites hear a word of hope in the midst of their captivity. God will restore their present circumstances. Paul's church lives out its faith by serving the Lord, using the gifts given to each individual by the Spirit. The disciples are called by Jesus. They accompany him to the wedding in Galilee. They respond to the sign at Cana by believing in Jesus and going out in ministry to the world. In our own faith, we respond to God's abundant, transforming grace by living out our gifts in service to the world.

The "sign" of Cana gives us this assurance: whatever challenges we face, Jesus's powerful grace can bring about transformation. Jesus is able to transform grief into joy. Jesus is able to transform poverty into abundance. Jesus is able to transform bitterness into love. We respond to the activity of God with belief and faith. And then we serve the needs of others by using the gifts God has given us.

Weddings are always crazy in one way or another. Something unexpected always happens. They also embody hope for the future. They affirm God's continued work in our midst in bringing together two individuals and transforming them into a couple. It's a common joke among groomsmen to chastise the groom about his life being over; but the reality is that life does change. Two become one. The hope we have is that a married couple embodies and reflects God's love for us and the world. Like the wedding at Cana, every wedding is a parable of God's abundant, overflowing grace. Married or not, may each of us live into the future and hope God has for us—one that is filled with possibility for belief and service. In the name of the Father, the Son, and the Holy Spirit, amen.

CHAPTER 2

A Gospel of a Different Color

When I introduce John to others, I like to start with a game. List some favorite stories of Jesus. Or said another way, what are some of the most well-known stories of Jesus? Here some usual responses:

- The Sermon on the Mount
- The healing stories
- The parables

Well, in John there is no Sermon on the Mount and no parables. However one could argue that many of John's stories have lessons beyond the story. So they are parabolic in that sense. Another fun John trivia game: What well-known stories are absent, besides the Sermon on the Mount? One would expect stories of Jesus to tell us of his nativity, but John does not (nor does Mark, for that matter). John's understanding of

Jesus's origins goes back much further, to a stable in Bethlehem, all the way to a time before the dawn of creation! John also does not include:

- The story of Jesus's baptism (it is referred to but not narrated, as in the other gospels)
- The temptation of Jesus
- The transfiguration of Jesus
- The institution of the Lord's Supper
- Jesus's painful experience on the cross

On the other hand, John does include stories from the other gospels, often with a unique perspective. There are only a couple of stories John has in common with the other evangelists (not counting the passion or the resurrection stories, although these also have unique Johannine perspectives): the cleansing of the temple and the feeding of a large crowd.

Several significant themes can be found throughout the gospel that help us understand John's perspective:

- The transition from the old way of understanding God to a new way, revealed in Jesus Christ
- The movement from the religious to the political

- The extravagance of God's grace
- The physical to the spiritual

And then there are the stories and themes unique to John; these shed light on the community's theological understanding. Only in John do we find:

- The wedding at Cana
- The visit of Nicodemus to Jesus at night
- The encounter of Jesus with the Samaritan woman at the well
- The raising of Lazarus from the dead
- The "I am" sayings of Jesus
- Washing the Disciples' feet on the night before Jesus's death

But what makes John stand out the most—making it a gospel of another color— is his description of the character and actions of Jesus. There is no "messianic secret" in John. Jesus never warns anyone (disciples, demons, etc.) to say anything about who he is. He is very open to sharing who he is with everyone. Jesus is centrally focused on his mission and does not put up barriers to those he is trying to save. There are no parables, no secrets, and no surprises. There is no hint of rethinking the mission, no hesitation, and even no suffering from the cross. Jesus understands the cross as the moment where he comes to his glory and the place where all people will be drawn to him. So his death is triumphant—a king on his throne—rather than an event of shame and defeat.

Throughout the gospel, we hear these words of invitation from Jesus or the disciples: "Come and see." The reader is also invited to come and see what Jesus is up to in this most unique account of his ministry. This driving force behind Jesus's words and actions is at the heart of every conversation he has. Even interactions with those whose intentions Jesus knows are hostile have a hint of invitation to them. This invitation extends to the reader of the gospel. Jesus's mission flows from the page to the heart of the one faithfully engaged with the text.

As we explore what makes the Gospel of John unique, a good first step is to examine what familiar stories of Jesus are included or excluded. If a story is found to be common among all four gospels, does John add a unique perspective? If a familiar story is absent, how does the absence add or subtract from John's understanding of Jesus? This is not meant to be an exhaustive list of everything John has in common with the other gospels, nor do I include every item unique to the fourth gospel. The stories included here are meant to give us a glimpse into the unique understanding of Jesus found in John, as compared to the other gospel accounts.

Omissions: Well-known Stories of Jesus from the Synoptic Gospels Not Found in John

Nativity (Matthew 2; Luke 1)

Shepherds, wise men, a star, the journey to Egypt: these are elements of the Christmas story we are used to hearing in December of every year. But John understood Jesus's roots to originate not with a virgin birth but from a time before the very beginning of creation. "In the beginning was the Word, and the Word was with God, and the Word was God" (John 1:1). Throughout the prologue (the first eighteen verses of the gospel), God's Word is not only understood by John to be the Holy Scriptures. John uses the Greek word *logos*, translated as "word," to describe Jesus—not in the sense of the words you are reading from this page but in the sense that Jesus was the very embodiment of God. Jesus is God's Word. This Word became flesh and lived among us.

John's origin story of Jesus goes back further in time than Bethlehem—to the beginning of time and all things. We understand that Jesus's roots are not in a human family and are not limited to time and space. Jesus's roots in God are timeless. From the very beginning of all things, Jesus was with God and was God. This almost cosmological understanding of Jesus contrasts with the cuteness of the nativity scenes that adorn our homes and churches in December. Our eyes and hearts are solely focused on the miracle of incarnation—the Creator of the universe come among the creation in a new way.

Even though Jesus's origin story does not include reference to Mary, Joseph, Bethlehem, Herod, or any of the other familiar elements of the Christmas narrative, the *Revised Common Lectionary* has appropriately assigned John 1:1–14 to be read on Christmas Day so that the best meaning of Jesus's incarnation is experienced. Lighted candle in hand, I have often read, "The light shines in the darkness, and the darkness did not overcome it" (John 1:5) at the close of Christmas Eve services as a benediction. In fact, my pulpit Bible has remnants of wax on that page.

From the beginning of the gospel, we learn that Jesus's origins precede the moment of creation and that Jesus is begotten of the Father, meaning, *of the same substance*. This relationship has an intimacy exemplified in 1:18: "No one has ever seen God; the only Son, who is in the heart of the Father, has made him known." That same relationship will be extended to all humanity through the love and grace of Jesus Christ. His mission—to offer salvation to all people—is very clear throughout the gospel. As his followers, we have an opportunity to fully share in his life, just as he shares in the Father's life. At the core of Jesus's ministry in John is an invitation to deeper love and meaning.

For the Preacher and Teacher

What are the implications for an alternative understanding of Jesus's origins? Is the message of Christmas enhanced or diminished because of John's different perspective? And how will hearers experience Christmas in a new way? Will the absence of a star and magi and shepherds impact how folk hear the story? What different understanding of incarnation ("Emmanuel, God with us" of the Synoptic Gospels) does John offer with "In the beginning was the Word … and the Word became flesh and dwelt among us"?

Baptism of Jesus (Matthew 3:13–17; Mark 1:9–11; Luke 3:21–22)

The Synoptic Gospels include accounts of Jesus's baptism by John the Baptist in the Jordan River. The Gospel of John only includes a fleeting reference. John the Baptist said, "I saw the Spirit descending from heaven like a dove, and it remained on him" (1:32). The other gospel accounts of Jesus's baptism contain a voice from the heavens announcing Jesus's identity to the crowds (Matthew 3:17) or a personal affirmation from God to Jesus (Mark 1:11; Luke 3:22). John may well understand such a proclamation of affirmation as redundant, since Jesus is to be the revealed Word of God. His identity was established before the very creation of all things. In the church, we understand the sacrament of baptism to be an outward and visible sign of an inward and spiritual grace. It is the once-in-a-lifetime proclamation of our identity in Christ. Through our baptism, we are forever identified with him.

For the Preacher and Teacher

Is a recorded experience of Jesus's baptism necessary for our understanding? Is a passing reference to his baptism enough? What are the implications of the absence of narrative about Jesus's baptism?

The Temptation of Jesus

The Synoptic Gospels offer accounts of Jesus's temptation by Satan (Matthew 4:1–11; Mark 1:12–13; Luke 4:1–13). Following his baptism, the Spirit, which alighted upon Jesus, compels him to go into the wilderness where he prepares for his ministry. After forty days of fasting, Jesus is tempted by Satan. His testing proves him worthy of his mission and serves as a springboard for his work as the Messiah of God. John, however, moves from the fleeting reference to Jesus's baptism to the calling of Jesus's disciples.

For the Preacher and Teacher

John offers no recollection of Jesus's wilderness experience, and Mark only summarizes it. Matthew and Luke build narratives around it, but their order of events is different. What do we learn about Jesus's ministry from this story? And what is left unlearned by its absence from John? Are these narratives necessary to introduce us to Jesus, or is what we glean from John's prologue (1:1–14) enough?

Additions: Stories and Lessons Only Found in John

The "I Am" Sayings of Jesus

A shepherd was out tending his sheep one day when he came upon an interesting sight: a bush on fire, but it was not being consumed by the flames. Curious, he investigated further. "Moses," he heard a voice say, "I have observed the misery of my people who are in Egypt. So come, I will send you to Pharaoh to bring my people the Israelites out of Egypt" (Exodus 3:7). Moses had never heard the voice of God before; indeed, this is the first time that God speaks in the Bible since the Jacob stories of the book of Genesis. Desperate for an excuse to stay with his family and flock, Moses resists and says, "If I come to the Israelites and say to them, 'The God of your ancestors has sent me to you,' and they ask, 'What is his name?' What shall I say to them?" (3:13). "God said to Moses, 'I am who I am.'" "He said further, 'Thus you shall say to the Israelites, I AM has sent me to you.' God also said to Moses, 'The Lord, the God of your ancestors, the God of Abraham, the God of Isaac, and the God of Jacob, has sent me to you'" (3:14, 15).

For the first time in Scripture, the divine name is revealed to a person—Moses, of all people—a murderer who fled justice. God's name is held in high regard in Judaism and Christianity, and its use is restricted, if not outright forbidden. To invoke God's name or to align oneself with God was considered blasphemy by the religious authorities in Jesus's day. The Gospel of John features the unique characteristic of the "I am" sayings of Jesus. For the overly religious who are already hostile to Jesus's teaching, the use of this term is gasoline to their fire. By the end of chapter 2 in the Gospel of John, following the cleansing of the temple, Jesus is already in trouble with the religious leaders. For the remainder of the gospel, his continual use of the phrase "I am" gets him into more and more danger. This includes even beginning a sentence with the words "I am."

In the Synoptic Gospels, Jesus is often careful to maintain a sense of anonymity, commonly referred to as the messianic secret: "Jesus went on with his disciples to the villages of Caesarea Philippi; and on the way he asked his disciples, 'Who do people say that I AM?' And they answered him, 'John the Baptist; and others Elijah; and still others one of the prophets.' He asked them, 'But who do you say that I AM?' Peter answered him, 'You are the Messiah.' And he sternly ordered them not to tell anyone about him" (Mark 8:27–30).

Jesus has no such concern about others learning his identity in the book of John. In fact, he reveals his identity over and over again to anyone who will listen. His use of the term "I am" is an intentional invocation of God's name. For example, in the Greek text, Jesus says to the Samaritan woman at the well, "I AM, the one who is speaking to you" (4:26). Note that English translations of the Bible translate this sentence "I am he" for grammatical reasons. By doing this, the deeper theological meaning of the Greek text is lost. The same thing happens several times:

- As Jesus walks on the water toward the disciples, struggling in the boat during the storm, "I AM;" he says. "Do not be afraid" (6:19). In Greek, Jesus does not say, "It is I," as our English translations would have us believe.

- "I told you that you would die in your sins, for you will die in your sins unless you believe that I AM" (8:24). "When you have lifted up the Son of Man, then you will realize that "I AM" (8:28).

- "Very truly I tell you, before Abraham was, I AM" (8:58).

- When Jesus is arrested in the garden, he says, "I AM," and the powerful soldiers fall to the ground (18: 5–6, 8).

Come on, English editors, give us the full theology—not just a footnote at the bottom of the page. We can handle it!

Following the multiplication of a child's lunch, used to feed thousands by the sea, Jesus says,

- "I am the Bread of Life. Whoever comes to me will never be hungry, and whoever believes in me will never be thirsty" (6:35, 48).

Light and darkness are continual themes throughout the gospel, beginning with verse four in chapter 1. Darkness is a central element in the conversation with Nicodemus (chapter 3) and Judas's betrayal of Jesus (chapter 13). Jesus's indictment of unbelievers is that they prefer darkness to the light because their deeds are evil. He says, "For all who do evil hate the light and do not come to the light, so that their deeds may not be exposed. But those who do what is true come to the light, so that it may be clearly seen that their deeds have been done in God" (3:20–21).

- "I am the Light of the World. Whoever follows me will never walk in darkness but will have the light of life" (8:12)

Many prominent biblical characters were shepherds (Moses, David). Shepherd is an ancient metaphor for God (Psalm 23; Ezekiel 34). Jesus identifies with this metaphor and uses it to expand his mission: to find other sheep not yet within his flock. He says, "I have other sheep that do not belong to this fold. I must bring them also, and they will listen to my voice. So there will be one flock, and one shepherd" (10:16–17). In his first resurrection appearance, Mary Magdalene recognizes Jesus only when he speaks her name (20:16), as the sheep recognize the voice of their shepherd.

- "I am the Gate for the sheep" (10:7, 9).
- "I am the Good Shepherd. The Good Shepherd lays down his life for the sheep" (10:11, 14).

Jesus invokes this "I am" teaching in the midst of a theological debate on the subject of death and resurrection of the faithful. We commonly invoke this teaching at funerals and memorial services.

- "I am the Resurrection and the Life. Those who believe in me, even though they die, will live, and whoever lives and believes in me will never die" (11:25).

Entire books have been written on this one verse. No, Jesus does not invalidate other religions with this teaching, and he does not condemn unbelievers to hell. They are simply sheep not of his own fold, and he continually seeks them out through his love and grace. Jesus's mission is to draw more and more people to him, and these words are an invitation to those who lack meaning in their lives. Jesus offers all unbelievers a path to salvation; he does not exclude anyone.

- "I am the way, and the truth, and the life. No one comes to the Father except through me" (14:6).

Offered during the farewell discourse (chapters 13 through 17), this "I am" teaching offers a model for the church's relationship to Jesus.

- "I am the True Vine/I am the Vine, you are the branches" (15:1, 5).

For the Preacher and Teacher

What is at stake in Jesus's repeated use of the "I am" phrase? Place yourself in the mind of Jesus's critics. How do you respond to blasphemy? What is at stake for them when Jesus self-identifies with God? What is lost when English translations change the Greek text from "I am" to "I am he" or "It is I"?

Stories Unique to John

The Wedding at Cana (John 2:1–12)

Jesus, his mother, and his disciples are at a wedding in Cana in Galilee. We learn that the supply of wine has run out, and Jesus's mother tells the staff that her son can help. Jesus objects to his mother's intervention. Many do not appreciate his addressing her as "woman." But this is not meant to be disrespectful; it is a term he uses throughout the gospel for his mother and other faithful women. This is the first time in John we hear reference to Jesus's "hour" or "time." It is an important key to understanding John's Christology. Jesus's hour or time refers to his coming to glory on the cross.

Despite Jesus's protests, he does help. He instructs the staff to fill six large jars with water. The narrator tells us these jars were used for the purpose of Jewish renewal cleansing, a ritual with which the Christian sacrament of baptism shares roots. The jars, we are told, are empty. This detail introduces us to one of John's core themes: changing from the former to the new. Vessels once used for

Jewish rituals are found empty, just as the lives of many of Jesus's religious opponents are empty. At Jesus's instructions, the jars are filled. And not just halfway or mostly full; the jars are filled to the brim.

The steward then retrieves the water, which has been transformed into wine. But it's not just any ordinary wine; it is of the highest quality. For a gospel without parables, this comes closest to being one. The overabundance of wine reminds us of God's love and grace, poured out for us through Jesus Christ. It is more than we ask, need, or imagine, and our access to it is immediate. God does not supply the minimum required but a super abundance. We are told the jars can hold up to thirty gallons of water each, meaning that Jesus has produced nearly 200 gallons of wine.

For the Preacher and Teacher

How do we experience grace? Does God supply only grace needed for the moment, or is God's grace abundant? Consider the impact of grace on your life. What signs have you experienced that point to Jesus's identity? What about your origins of faith? What did you "see and believe" that brought you to faith? Have you stopped looking for signs?

The Conversation with Nicodemus (John 3:1–21)

Nicodemus personifies the Jewish leaders of Jesus's day. He is not named as one of the overly zealous opponents of Jesus, even though he was a member of the Sanhedrin (a religious body comprised of many Jewish leaders). The Sanhedrin ultimately found Jesus guilty of blasphemy. Nicodemus is present at the burial of Jesus, bringing with him an abundant offering of spices (19:39). We are told by the narrator that the visit came "by night," a note most folk presume to be some kind of anonymous cover—visiting Jesus at night to avoid being noticed by the other Jewish authorities. But there is more to this than an afterthought. Nicodemus is spiritually in the dark as well, and Jesus is the Light of the World, as well as the true light from John's prologue. So the visit has an undertone of exploration rather than curiosity. And Jesus's responses are filled with invitation in the hope that Nicodemus will become a disciple.

Nicodemus refers to Jesus as "rabbi" (teacher) and then: "we [the religious leaders] know you are a teacher from God, for no one can do these signs that you do apart from the presence of God" (3:2). Jesus responds with this invitation: "No one can enter the kingdom of God without being born from above" (3:3). Nicodemus is confused by this and responds with a question about an old man reentering his mother's womb. Nicodemus does not understand the invitational nature of Jesus's words.

In John, people often become confused when speaking to Jesus. It isn't that his message is difficult to comprehend—it's just unexpected. And it is not uncommon for us to think rationally and logically about situations or issues we do not fully understand. Jesus aims to break through our initial resistance and confusion and invite us into further relationship with him.

Again, his mission is about inviting people to something new. In the exchange with Nicodemus, he invited not only Nicodemus to this new relationship with God; he invited all of Nicodemus's fellow Jewish leaders. Jesus uses the word "you" over and over again: "You must be born from above;" "You do not receive my testimony;" "You do not believe." In English we cannot differentiate between singular and plural uses of the word "you." But in Greek there is a difference, and each "you" reference here is *plural*. Jesus seeks to win not only Nicodemus but others like him who find themselves in spiritual darkness. To the one who visited him at night Jesus says, "Light has come into the world, but people loved the darkness more because their deeds were evil" (3:19). We'll learn later that Jesus self-identifies as the Light of the World. But for now, as we move on from Nicodemus, it is enough to know that Jesus is calling him—and those who think and act like him—to move from darkness to light.

For the Preacher and Teacher

How do you understand the references to night and light? Was Nicodemus coming under cover of darkness to protect his identity, or is there more at stake? What impact does this conversation have on him? Do you think he became a disciple, or did he remain in his original understanding? If you could approach Jesus secretly or publicly, what would you ask? Why do think Nicodemus seeks out Jesus?

The Samaritan Woman (John 4:1–42)

The Samaritans and Israelites share a common history and ancestry, but along the way, a divorce happened. Centuries later, they each had their own centers of worship, established religious practices, and identity. There was a mutual hatred for the other. So when Jesus decided to return to Galilee from Judea, there was a way to make the trip and avoid Samaria. All Jews took that route. We are puzzled then when Jesus says he *"must* go through Samaria"

(4:4, italics added). Why must he go through there? He leaves us wondering and takes off, only to stop at the base of a well in the noonday sun. Then he has a surprising encounter with a woman who has come to draw water. We wonder why she chose the hottest time of day to do this; most women would go to the well early or late in the day. So we are immediately suspicious of her. Not only is she a Samaritan—she has something to hide.

Jesus asks for a drink, and she is shocked—so are we—that a Jewish man would ask a drink of a Samaritan woman. "How is it that you, a Jew, ask a drink of me?" But Jesus comes right back at her: "If you knew the one asking for a drink you would ask him for a drink, and he would offer you living water" (4:10). Invitation. The same invitation offered to Nicodemus under the cover of darkness is now offered to this woman in the light of the sun. Her response echoes Nicodemus's original response and those of Jesus's accusers in the temple in chapter 2. They are all centered on physical reality.

- Nicodemus: How can an old man reenter his mother's womb?
- Religious leaders: How can you rebuild this temple in three days when we've been working on it for half a century?

- Woman at the well: Where is your bucket? How can you offer me living water if you can't draw water out of the well?
- Later at the tomb of Lazarus (chapter 11): We can't roll away the stone. He's been dead three days; the stench will be terrible!

People struggle with Jesus's message. Sometimes they are confused because of its newness; others are threatened by it. So when challenging or seeking deeper understanding, they resort to well-established realities. What is known is tangible reality. It can be touched, smelled, felt. The unfamiliar understanding Jesus calls us to creates confusion and anxiety. Jesus calls us to seek beyond the limits of a rational, understandable world and find the deeper meaning God leads us to.

So the woman goes to a different rational place: "Are you greater than our ancestor Jacob, who gave us the well...?" (4:12) *Our ancestor.* She is calling upon the shared history of Jews and Samaritans— before they divorced into two different faiths. Are you greater than what we know is an authentic, ancient, covenantal relationship with God?

What Jesus offers is more than the religious traditions of the past. The bread Jesus offers in

Chapter 6 and the water he offers in chapter 4 are better. They are so much better that one may eat and drink of them and never grow hungry or thirsty again. As great as those traditions are, one must still gather the manna every day because it does not keep overnight. And the well is the only source of water for this Samaritan city of Sychar. Hear the words of invitation from Jesus: "The water I give will become in them a spring of water gushing up to eternal life" (4:14).

The hook is baited. She nibbles: "Sir, give me this water, so that I may never be thirsty or have to keep coming here to draw water" (4:15). She is closer to understanding; she sees Jesus as one who offers water. But it's still the kind of water one draws from a well. Then Jesus turns the tables on her, mentioning her complicated personal life. Perhaps now we know a little more about why she comes to the well at noon rather than the cool of the morning or evening. Maybe she has grown tired of the accusatory looks of the other women of the village. "Sir, I see that you are a prophet," (4:19) she says, noting Jesus's ability to see into her life. Then she falls into the old trap of Jew vs. Samaritan: "Our ancestors worshipped on this mountain, but you say the place people must worship is in Jerusalem" (4:20). "Woman, believe me," Jesus begins. *Believe me.* "The hour is coming when you will worship the Father neither on this mountain nor in Jerusalem" (4:21). Drawing on her religious traditions, she says, "I know that Messiah is coming" (4:25). "I am he," Jesus says, as it is translated in English. The original Greek test simply says, "I AM," the name of God (4:26).

Just at this revelatory moment, the disciples return from wherever they had traveled to and are alarmed to see Jesus speaking to a woman in public. While Jesus tends to their emotional state, the woman leaves behind her water jar and returns to the town. She walks throughout the city, calling to anyone who will listen. The same woman who came to the well at noon to avoid human contact now actively seeks it out: "Come and see [John's signature phrase of evangelistic invitation] a man who told me everything I have ever done. He cannot be the Messiah, can he?" (4:29). The Samaritans come to the well. They invite this Jewish teacher to remain with them for three days. The enemy has become a houseguest, and many lives are changed.

Now we know why Jesus used the word "must" when describing his travel plans from Judea to Galilee. Of course he did not have to go through Samaria to get home. There were plenty of safer routes. But going the usual way would achieve the usual results: Samaritans would remain outsiders to the new thing God was doing. He had to go through Samaria to find this particular woman. He had to go through Samaria to speak to this particular village. Because of his detour, many others heard the good news. Jesus's "must" is linked to his mission—to draw *all people* to him.

For the Preacher and Teacher

How do you traditionally understand this story? What new understanding has surfaced? How is evangelism linked to your ministry—through sermons or lessons? What opportunities are offered so that others "come and see" Jesus through your ministry and life? What barriers have you constructed to keep others out and yourself locked in? What tired arguments do you habitually arouse to maintain the status quo? It can be argued that this woman became one of Jesus's first evangelists. She actively brought others to him. Do you recall a similar impact on your own life after hearing the gospel? Are new people experiencing conversion through your ministry? How is their witness impacting the community?

The Raising of Lazarus (John 11:1–44)

This story is unique because of the intimate relationships Jesus shared with Lazarus, Mary, and Martha—brother and sisters to each other and dear friends of Jesus. So it is personal.

At the end of chapter 10, the disciples and Jesus leave Judea under difficult circumstances. They are in the relative peace of the wilderness near the Jordan River when news arrives of Lazarus's serious illness. [Note: This is a different Lazarus than the one in Luke 16:19–31.] Although his friend is deathly ill, Jesus decides to remain in the wilderness for a few extra days. When he announces it is time to return to Judea, the disciples object, knowing they will find more hostility there. Thomas sums up the situation: "Let us all go, that we may die with him" (11:16).

Upon his arrival, Jesus learns that Lazarus has indeed died. Martha and Mary's house is surrounded by wailing mourners. Martha runs out to the road to meet Jesus, saying, "Lord, if you had been here my brother would not have died. But even now I know that God will give you whatever you ask of him" (11:22). Jesus says, "Your brother will rise again" (11:23). Now Martha reaches back into her religious past, as so many others have done in this gospel. The woman at the well recalled Jacob; the religious folk in the synagogue recalled Moses; and Martha knows what she believes: "I know that he will rise again in the resurrection on the last day" (11:24). The latter is a reference to the belief in end-time resurrection held by some Jews. But as he did before, Jesus takes a former teaching and renews it: "I AM the resurrection and the life. Those who believe in me will never die. Do you believe this?" (11:26). Here again is an invitation—even to Martha, who knew Jesus well. She responds with a great affirmation of faith: "Yes, Lord, I believe you are the Messiah, the Son of God, the one coming into the world" (11:27).

Then Mary, the other sister, comes to meet Jesus, who has still not arrived at the graveside. Mary says the same thing, word for word, as her sister said to Jesus: "Lord, if you had been here my brother would not have died" (11:32). Then the narrator adds a striking comment: "When Jesus saw her weeping, and the others too, he was greatly disturbed in spirit and deeply moved" (11:33). Many readers of the story assume this is Jesus's own grief or compassion for those who are hurting. But I read the story in a different way; this is anger, not grief. Jesus is angry that so many have failed to understand his mission—including Mary and (as we'll see in a moment) Martha. If they truly believed, they would not be so resistant. "Where have you laid him?" Jesus asks in 11:34. "Lord, come and see." The same words used throughout the gospel for invitation is the response he hears.

Approaching the grave, we find the shortest Scripture in the Bible: "Jesus began to weep" (11:35). Why does Jesus weep? Is he overcome with grief or troubled by present circumstances? Does he weep for the apparent lack of faith in Mary and the surrounding mourners? In a gospel without parables, is this one? Is Jesus thinking of his own tomb, into which he will be laid in just a short time? At his weeping, those gathered at the cemetery murmured about it, even wondering aloud why Jesus didn't save Lazarus in the first place. As he comes near the tomb, we are told Jesus again is greatly disturbed. Upon hearing his instruction to remove the stone, Martha shows up again: "Lord, already there is a stench because he has been dead four days" (11:39). It's the same sort of natural physical reaction he has received from others, like Nicodemus ("must I re-enter my mother's womb?") and the Samaritan woman ("where is your bucket to draw the water from the well?"). But usually those who voice this resistance are outsiders, ones who do not understand who Jesus is or fully appreciate his mission. But Martha? She is the one who just voiced the great affirmation of her faith: "Yes, Lord I believe you are the Messiah." Yet Martha is concerned about the stench of her dead brother.

Grief is one of the most powerful emotions we can experience, and persons suffering from it often find their most fundamental ways of seeing the world changed. The doubt, the questions of the onlookers and the proximity to his own death and burial are at the heart of Jesus's anger. Note the details of the scene as Lazarus appears from the grave: the stone rolled away, the formerly dead man wearing burial cloths. It is impossible to believe Lazarus's death and his resurrection are not connected to Jesus's own (chapter 20).

Stories in Common with the Synoptic Gospels

Matthew, Mark, and Luke, for the most part, share their stories of Jesus and follow a similar sequence of events. This is why they are referred to as "synoptic." Each evangelist has his own unique stories, and Matthew and Luke share stories not found in Mark. What is striking about John is that this gospel only shares two stories with the other gospels, outside of the passion and resurrection of Jesus. And within those stories, the details and tone are radically different. John shares with the others the cleansing of the temple and the feeding of a large crowd. But each story is tailored to fit within the established themes of the gospel.

The Cleansing of the Temple (2:13–25)

The cleansing of the temple is found in all four gospels (Matthew 21:12–17; Mark 11:15–19; Luke 19:45–48; John 2:13–25). The Synoptic Gospels locate the temple episode at the beginning of the passion narrative, the last week of Jesus's life. Matthew, Mark, and Luke precede the temple story with Jesus's triumphal entry into Jerusalem, traditionally read on Palm Sunday, the Sunday before Easter. Crowds line the streets; people wave their palm branches in the air and shout, "Hosanna to the Son of David!" (Matthew 21:9). The scene is filled with references to Old Testament imagery of the promised Messiah arriving gloriously. These same crowds, just a few days later, will be the ones to shout, "Crucify him!" The difference with John is its location (in chapter 2) and the fact that John separates this story from Jesus's triumphal entry into Jerusalem (found in chapter 12). Jesus is hardly known by anyone who wasn't present for the sign at the wedding in Cana, which immediately precedes this story.

Jesus inaugurates a new understanding of God's revelation to humanity. One of the challenges religious folk have is a resistance to new ways of experiencing God. Jesus always confronted this resistance with a radical invitation. One of the major themes of the fourth gospel is the conflict between Jesus and the religious leaders of his day. John's use of "the Jews" as an all-inclusive term for Jesus's opponents has led some to anti-Semitic actions and beliefs; but John does not condemn Judaism. In fact, Jesus is seen as the renewing of Jewish faith. John's criticism of religious folk is about their blindness (chapter 9) to the new thing God is doing in Jesus. They would rather protect their traditions and institutions and their established ways of worship and practice than consider a new alternative. The conflict becomes more and more acute as the gospel moves forward, but Jesus's rebuttals are best understood as an invitation to a new way of worship and experience— not judgment or exclusion.

King Solomon built the first temple roughly 1,000 years before the time of Jesus; it was then destroyed by the Babylonians in 587 BCE. It was rebuilt roughly a century later and then renovated by Herod the Great. The temple symbolized God's presence among the people until it was ultimately destroyed by the Romans in 70 CE. The temple in Jerusalem was the center of Jewish worship. What Jesus finds there is very disturbing to him. He sees that the religious practices of Judaism—his own practices—have become corrupt and empty. They have grown stale and lifeless, institutionalized and separated from God. Jesus overturns the tables and ties several cords together to form a whip. He shouts, "Destroy this Temple and in three days I will raise it up" (2:19). The religious leaders who were present scoff at this notion. Their response is rooted in physical reality: they have been working on this temple for decades. How can one obscure teacher rebuild it over a weekend? Jesus, we know, is not interested in the building as much as what it represents, and it has come to represent stale religious practices. The leaders' first instinct is to protect their institution and their form of worship. The narrator informs us that Jesus is referring to his body.

Why does John include the story in chapter 2 rather than chapters 18 or 19, where the passion story begins? Because John sets the stage for the religious conflict Jesus will face throughout his ministry at the beginning—not the end. The synoptic writers place the temple cleansing near the end to set the stage for the passion of Jesus. The religious leaders' violent reaction to Jesus's antics there led directly to his crucifixion.

For the Preacher and Teacher

The cleansing of the temple is recorded in all four gospels, yet John's placement of the story is very different. Rather than at the beginning of the passion of Jesus, John narrates the temple story in chapter 2. Why is this important? What institutions today might Jesus denounce, and how do we defend them? What spiritual practices are so important that they blind us to the new thing God is inaugurating around us? How do we keep ourselves attuned to what God is doing?

The Feeding of a Large Crowd (John 6:1–71)

This, along with the temple cleansing, is another story common to all four gospels. In fact, Matthew and Mark record it twice, so count it six times in four gospels! (Matthew 14:13–21, 15:32–39; Mark 6:30–44, 8:1–10; Luke 9:10–17). The difference between the synoptic accounts and John's is what happens next. The other gospels understand the feeding of a large crowd as another miracle of Jesus. The next day, it is on to something else. John continues the story into the next day, as a setting for yet another argument with the religious leaders.

Jesus asks Philip, "Where are we to buy bread for these people?" (6:5). His response is familiar—a rational, measurable number: "Six months' wages would not buy enough for each of them to get a little" (6:7). Jesus then does the familiar: he takes bread, blesses it, multiplies it, and serves it to the people. It is a eucharistic moment by the sea. The people see the event and understand it as a "sign," like changing water into wine at the wedding in chapter 2. And, echoing the woman at the well in chapter 4, they say, "This is indeed the prophet who is to come into the world." So they see something in Jesus beyond the magical—at least for the moment.

Following the feeding of the large crowd, the disciples cross the sea. While they are out there, a violent storm surrounds them. Jesus comes to them, and they are terrified. In English translations, Jesus says, "It is I. Do not be afraid" (6:20). But like the story of the woman in chapter 4, the Greek text has Jesus say, "I AM," not "It is I," so that he is identified with God. The following morning, Jesus and his disciples are found on the other side of the lake. An argument breaks out between Jesus and his religious opponents over the nature of one's relation to God. "Rabbi, when did you get here? What sign will you give us, so that we may see and believe?" (6:25). Jesus knows their spiritual state: "You are looking for me, not because you saw signs but because you ate your fill of bread. Do not work for the food that perishes but for the food that endures for eternal life, which the Son of Man will give to you" (6:26–27).

His response takes us back to the woman at the Samaritan well. Her ancestors drew water from that well, and they have returned for more every day. Drink from Jesus's living water, and never return to the well again. Here, the invitation is given to eat of a different sort of bread than what they expect. And like the woman, their initial response is to go back in time, further away from the situation: "What are you going to give us then, that we may see it and believe you? Our ancestors ate the bread in the wilderness" (6:30). The woman initially transports back in time to Jacob, who dug the well. By the sea, Jesus's opponents transport back to Moses and the exodus.

Jesus attempts to bring them forward in time; note the verb tenses. "It was not Moses who *gave* you the bread from heaven, but it is my Father who *gives* you the true bread of heaven" (author's emphasis; 6:32). Again echoing the Samaritan woman, they say, "Sir, give us this bread always" (6:34). But Jesus makes it personal: "I AM the Bread of Life. Whoever comes to me will never be hungry and whoever believes in me will never be thirsty" (6:35). But before they respond, he goes beyond this argument to reveal the overall mission: "This is indeed the will of my Father, that all who see the Son and believe in him may have eternal life; and I will raise them up on the last day" (6:40).

Jesus speaks of himself as bread that has come down from heaven, but the authorities mention the bread of the exodus as what God provided to feed Israel. Jesus says, "Your ancestors ate the manna in the wilderness and they died. This is the bread that comes down from heaven, so that one may eat of it and not die" (6:50).

Religious folk often look to the events of the past to better understand the events of the present. Years ago, I served a couple of churches in Britain, and I remember the fondness of the memories folk had of a Sunday school anniversary from decades before: children dressed in white, packing the balcony full. It was not a denial of the present or a condemnation of the future but a special memory. Jesus's opponents, however, are stuck. They seem to live in such a memory, disregarding what God is currently doing in their midst. Jesus says, "It was not Moses who gave [past tense] the bread but your Father who gives [present tense] bread." Again, these are not words of judgment but of invitation. Like Nicodemus' visit at night, Jesus knows the spiritual condition of his rivals, and he invites them to transformation. And some of them cannot accept it; even some anonymous disciples fall away.

For the Preacher and Teacher

What inhibits our ability to see clearly what God is doing in our lives? How easy is it to transition into defense mode when our traditionally-held views are challenged? Do you have "line in the sand" ideas about God that can never be crossed? How do we know the difference between a legitimate challenge and a point of view that better informs our understanding?

Jesus Anointed with Oil (12:1–8)

This story is recorded by all four gospel writers, or at least there is a similar account in all four gospels. Matthew and Mark place the anointing within the passion story, immediately before the Last Supper (Matthew 26:6–13; Mark 14:3–9). Interestingly, Luke breaks with his synoptic brothers to place it early in the gospel (7:36–50). It is found in John midway through the gospel. Matthew and Mark understand the anointing as a prelude for Jesus's burial. The women who come Sunday morning to anoint Jesus's body after his death on the cross the previous Friday are too late; he has already risen from grave. But it doesn't matter because his body was previously anointed.

The disciples protest, claiming the money could have been used for the poor, but Jesus responds with, "You will always have the poor with you; but you do not always have me" (12:8). Mark adds the point that the disciples scolded the anonymous woman. Matthew and Mark end their version of the story with Jesus pronouncing, "Truly I tell you, wherever this good news is proclaimed in the whole world, what she has done will always be told *in remembrance of her*" (author's emphasis; Mark 14:9; Matthew 26:13), a hint of eucharistic language. Unfortunately, we remember her act but not her name. Luke understands this gracious act to be about forgiveness. The woman is identified as a "woman of the city, a sinner" (Luke 7:37). While weeping, she anoints Jesus's feet, not his head, and Jesus uses the gift as a metaphor to challenge his host's lack of hospitality. He pronounces her sins forgiven, which leads to grumbling around the table. There are no self-righteous pronouncements from the disciples about the outrageous expense of the gesture.

John takes the details from all three accounts and blends them. The story is found midway through the gospel in chapter 12—not in the house of the Pharisee Simon but in Lazarus's home. And the woman who anoints Jesus is not anonymous at all; it is Mary, the sister of Lazarus and Martha (11:1–44). As in Luke's account, it is Jesus's feet that are anointed, not his head. Unlike Matthew and Mark, it is not "the disciples" who gripe about the enormous expense. It is Judas Iscariot who will betray Jesus later in the gospel. John adds the detail that Judas was motivated to object, not out of a sense of justice but greed: "He was a thief; he kept the common purse and used to steal what was put into it" (12:6). John retains the detail that the gift was meant for his burial, as well as the teaching about the omnipresence of the poor. One detail unique to John is "the house was filled with the fragrance of the perfume" (12:3).

This statement reminds us of the overabundance of grace at the wedding of Cana. The water changed to wine was not simply enough to get through the shortage; it was more than anyone could possibly drink. The gift of the perfume is so powerful that it is enjoyed by more than those closest to Jesus. Everyone in the entire house can appreciate Mary's generosity.

Over the centuries, interpreters of this story merged the details so that the woman was identified as Mary Magdalene. This cut-and-paste approach to interpretation is rooted in John's naming of the woman as "Mary," the sister of Lazarus (12:3), Luke's note of a woman "of the city, a sinner," (7:37), and his introduction of Mary Magdalene as one previously healed of many demons (8:2). Never, in any gospel, is Mary Magdalene explicitly identified as the woman who anoints Jesus; nor, contrary to another ancient rumor, is she ever described as a former prostitute.

For the Preacher and Teacher

The other stories common to the four gospels—the cleansing of the temple and the feeding of a large crowd—were certainly grand enough to remember. What makes this story so memorable? What unique spin does each writer give to the story, given its details and placement in the gospel? How do you understand this story? How does John's identification of the woman as Mary change your view? Why does John single out Judas as the one who complains about the expense of the ointment?

A Sermon

Like the abundant grace witnessed at the wedding of Cana in the changing of water to wine, the smell of the perfume offered to Jesus fills the entire house. This sermon challenges us to live our lives in such a way that we are a fragrant offering to the Lord.

"A Sweet Smelling Offering"
Ephesians 4:25–5:2 (John 12:1–6 referenced)
First Sunday of Advent
November 29, 2015

Today we begin a new sermon series for Advent entitled "The Gift." Each week, we will reflect on one of the gifts presented to the Christ child by the magi. Most of us are very familiar with the story, as it is found in chapter 2 of Matthew, so I'll briefly summarize it. Wise men, or magi "from the East" notice an unusual star in the heavens. Perhaps they are astrologers. They decide to follow the star. They enter Israel, and as is the custom of the day, they visit Herod, the king of the Jews, to announce their travel intentions. They ask, "Where is the one born King of the Jews?" Herod has no idea but asks the magi to return to him and give the location once they find the child. They follow the star until it rests above Bethlehem. They offer their gifts of gold, frankincense, and myrrh, and they return home. They are never heard from again, but their gifts to the child endure in our collective Christmas memory.

Now, why I was assigned frankincense to speak about I do not know, other than my name is Frank, or it has the least amount of biblical material to support the subject. Gold was traditionally offered as a gift to royalty. Myrrh may have had medicinal properties. One of the gospels tells us Jesus was offered wine mixed with myrrh as he suffered on the cross—not to remedy his pain but to prolong his suffering.

This past week was Thanksgiving, and perhaps you burned a few candles in your home to sweeten the aroma of the place before the arrival of your guests. Frankincense is a spice that is burned, producing a sweet smell. In biblical times, it was very expensive, so only the wealthy were able to use it. It was commonplace in ancient times to burn frankincense in the presence of royalty. Its smell testified to the power and authority present in the guests. It was commonly burned in the presence of Roman emperors, who were considered gods by their subjects. Frankincense also had religious properties. When burned during worship as a sacrifice, it again announced the presence of a mighty and powerful God.

In ancient Israel, sacrifice was a vital element of Jewish worship. Animals and spices were often offered as burnt offerings in the temple of Jerusalem or at local shrines if one was traveling. The first reference we have to a burnt offering follows the great flood. God makes a covenant with Noah to never again destroy the earth by water. As a sign of the covenant, Noah builds an altar and offers several animals as a burnt offering. We are told the smell was pleasing to God.

Throughout the early part of the Old Testament, burnt offerings were offered to God, and the smell was pleasing and acceptable. But after some time, worship became empty. People—then and now—offered worship as a ritual, something they had to do. Worship became clouded by the sins of idolatry and laziness. Suddenly, God refused to accept Israelite worship and said, "I will not smell your pleasing odors" (Leviticus 26:31). Chapter 1 of Isaiah details God's frustration with the brokenness of Israel's relationship with God: "What to me is the multitude of your sacrifices? says the Lord; I have had enough of burnt offerings of rams and the fat of fed beasts; I do not delight in the blood of bulls, or of lambs, or of goats. When you come to appear before me who asked this from your hand? Trample my courts no more; bringing offerings is futile; incense is an abomination to me" (Isaiah 1:11–13).

But ...

If we turn from our sinfulness, if we remember who we are and honor our covenant relationship with God, God will once again accept our offerings. His instructions are to "Wash yourselves clean; remove the evil of your doings from before my eyes; cease to do evil, learn to do good; seek justice, rescue the oppressed, defend the orphan, plead for the widow" (Isaiah 1:16–17). We can fix our relationship with God by recognizing our brokenness and repenting of our sins.

One of my favorite Bible stories is found in all four gospels—a very rare thing. It's the story of a woman who anoints Jesus's body before his death. In Matthew, Mark, and Luke, this woman is anonymous. But in John chapter 12, she is named: Mary of Bethany, the sister of Lazarus and Martha. After the raising from the dead of her brother, which happened in chapter 11, Mary hosts Jesus at her home. She breaks a jar of expensive perfume (not frankincense, but you get the idea) and pours it over Jesus's feet, drying them with her hair. The disciples self-righteously object, saying, "Why go to this expense? This money could have been used for the poor!" But Jesus says, "You will always have the poor with you, but you will not always have me." He accepts her extravagant gift, the smell of which fills the entire house. Our lives could be such a gracious offering to God, and the sweet smell could fill not only our houses or churches but the whole world.

Today we begin the season of Advent, the four weeks leading up to Christmas. Advent originally was thought of by the church as being similar to Lent, the forty days before Easter. These holy days were meant to be a time of preparation. For many of us today, Advent is simply a countdown to Christmas. Each day on Twitter, someone tweets, "Twenty-eight days until Christmas!" But I would offer this caution: slow down. Examine your life. Before the coming of Christmas, consider what roadblocks exist between you and God. We know God will not accept our offerings or worship if they are not offered with pure hearts. God knows our hearts, what brokenness there is in them. What is it for you? Is it ambition at work or school? Are you determined to get ahead, regardless of the consequences for those around you? Is it a lack of compassion for others in need? Is your first reaction to those less fortunate than you to encourage them to fix their own situations? Advent can be a time to put your relationship with God in a healthy place. A commitment to do so will make your celebration of Christmas even more joyful.

This past week, we did a ton of driving. My cousin was married in Las Vegas, and I had the privilege of presiding at the service. We drove because the boys are out of school for the entire week of Thanksgiving, so we took our time returning home. We stopped at Hoover Dam, the Grand Canyon, and we even saw the Meteor Crater in Arizona.

Driving through the mountains and hiking down a little way into the Grand Canyon, I was overwhelmed with the beauty of it all. It was my first trip. I could show you pictures, but they just do not do justice to the experience. Everything echoed God's glory and power. Here's the thing about the creation: it too, like us, suffers from sin. It's not the creation's fault—it is not capable of sin—but the state of sin that is transmitted to everything as a result of original sin. The apostle Paul said in Romans,

> For the creation waits with eager longing for the revealing of the children of God; for the creation was subjected to futility, not of its own will but by the will of the one who subjected it, in hope that the creation itself will be set free from its bondage to decay and will obtain the freedom of the glory of the children of God. We know that the whole creation

has been groaning in labor pains until now; and not only the creation, but we ourselves, who have the first fruits of the Spirit, groan inwardly while we wait for adoption, the redemption of our bodies. (Romans 8:19–23)

Advent is a time of waiting for redemption at the coming of Christ.

Our text for today, Ephesians 4:25–5:2, enjoins us to live our lives in such a way that they are pleasing to God.

So then, putting away falsehood, let all of us speak the truth to our neighbors, for we are members of one another. Be angry but do not sin; do not let the sun go down on your anger, and do not make room for the devil. Thieves must give up stealing; rather let them labor and work honestly with their own hands, so as to have something to share with the needy. Let no evil talk come out of your mouths, but only what is useful for building up, as there is need, so that your words may give grace to those who hear. And do not grieve the Holy Spirit

of God, with which you were marked
with a seal for the day of redemption.
Put away from you all bitterness and
wrath and anger and wrangling and
slander, together with all malice, and
be kind to one another, tender-hearted,
forgiving one another, as God in Christ
has forgiven you. Therefore be imitators
of God, as beloved children, and live
in love, as Christ loved us and gave
himself up for us, a fragrant offering
and sacrifice to God.

As Jesus lived his life as a fragrant offering before
the Lord, so you and I can. We can put away lies,
deceit, anger, stealing, and whatever else it is that
blocks us from God. We can be kind, tenderhearted,
forgiving, and loving, as Christ was and is.

The magi's trip into and out of Israel was quick,
but the gifts they offered—gold, frankincense, and
myrrh—had a lasting significance. So may our lives
be led in such a way that God is pleased with the
sweet smell. In the name of the Father, the Son, and
the Holy Spirit, amen.

CHAPTER 3

From Darkness to Light

Entrance into Jerusalem (12:12–44)

John's passion story begins, as the other gospels do, with Jesus's triumphant entry into Jerusalem at Passover. This is the third Passover recorded in John's gospel (2:23, 6:4). The crowds cut down palm branches from the trees and lay them before him, shouting, "Hosanna! Blessed is the one who comes in the name of the Lord, the King of Israel!" (12:13). While John has this introduction in common with the other gospel writers, very soon a new trail is followed. Jesus does not journey to the temple and "cleanse" it here, as he does in the Synoptics; he has already done that in chapter 2 of John. Instead, Jesus offers a variety of teachings to the disciples and others. Some Greeks in town for Passover wish to see Jesus, and the disciples convey the message to him. Instead of a yes or no, Jesus responds, "The hour has come for the Son of Man to be glorified" (12:23). The phrase "hour has come" reminds us of several sayings of Jesus throughout John, the first being at Cana, when Jesus protested his mother's intervention by saying, "My hour has not yet come" (2:4). What makes this particular moment, this particular Passover (of the three John remembered) Jesus's hour? Because the cross is now looming.

Again, John takes us in a different direction. The events and themes of the last few days of Jesus's life are well known to us, but they are almost exclusively derived from Matthew, Mark, or Luke:

- Jesus's triumphal entry into Jerusalem
- The cleansing of the temple
- Passover meal with the disciples
- Institution of the Lord's Supper
- Jesus's heartfelt struggle in the garden ("Take this cup from me ...")
- Jesus's humiliation at his trials and crucifixion
- Jesus's painful suffering on the cross, including his own words of desperation and isolation

But these elements are largely absent from John because John understands Jesus's passion in a different way. In fact, John would even object to our use of the word "passion," since it is derived from the Latin word for suffering. The passion of Jesus in John is anything but cruel; it is triumphant—the culmination of Jesus's entire ministry. We see this immediately following his entrance in to Jerusalem. The Greeks want to see him, but Jesus responds with teaching for the disciples:

- "Unless a grain of wheat falls to the earth and dies, it remains a single grain; but if it dies it bears much fruit" (12:24; cf. 1 Corinthians 15:36–38).
- "Those who love their life will lose it, and those who hate their life in this world will keep it for eternal life" (12:25; Matthew 10:39; Mark 8:35; Luke 17:33).
- "Whoever serves me must follow me, and where I am there my servant will be also. Whoever serves me, the Father will honor" (12:26; Mark 8:34).

These are not unfamiliar sayings of Jesus—they are echoed in other gospels—but *not in this context.* In Matthew, Mark, and Luke, these teachings are not found within the passion story but elsewhere, often couched between other random teachings. Why does John include them here? Next, Jesus really surprises us. Because of the synoptic influence on our knowledge of the story, we expect the question about a cup passing from Jesus to be part of a desperate prayer for divine intervention moments before his arrest in the garden. Not so in John. It's right here, following these teachings on discipleship: "Now my soul is troubled. What should I say—Father, save me from this hour? No, it is for this reason that I have come to this hour. Father glorify your name" (12:27–28). Then a voice from heaven responds, "I have glorified it, and I will glorify it again" (12:29). There is no struggle here, no anguish, and no second thoughts. Jesus is fully aware of his mission and his Father's will.

Then Jesus says, "This voice has come for your sake, not for mine. Now is the judgment of this world; now the ruler of this world will be driven out. And I, when I am lifted up from the earth, will draw all people to myself" (12:30–32). This is Jesus's core mission statement. The crowds who hear this teaching protest. Jesus's response is filled with the familiar invitation we have seen throughout John: "You will not have the light much longer. While the light is with you, walk in the light, so that the darkness will not overtake you. While you have the light, believe the light, so that you may become children of light" (12:35–36). A few verses later, Jesus continues, saying, "I have come as light to the world, so that everyone who believes in me should not remain in darkness. I do not judge anyone who hears my words and does not keep them, for I came not to judge the world, but to save the world" (12:44–50). Invitation, invitation, invitation.

For the Preacher and Teacher

Why are these differences between John and the other gospels so important? Are the missing elements essential to the story? Do you prefer the synoptic accounts or John's? Why? Why are the synoptic details most familiar to us? Does John's different perspective offer significant challenges to your understanding of the meaning of Jesus's passion?

The Farewell Discourse

Chapters 13 through 17 in John are unique to this gospel. Chapter 13 deals with a meal that Jesus shared with the disciples—but not as it is commonly understood. Chapters 14 through17 are prayers offered by Jesus in support of his beloved community, which is soon to be without its leader.

A Last Supper, Not *the* Last Supper (13:1–20)

Jesus does share a meal with his disciples, but it is not designated as a Passover seder. John is very clear that this meal happened *before* the Passover. So it makes sense that the Eucharist is not instituted here. John has another theological understanding of this meal to communicate to us. At the meal, and only in John, Jesus rises from the table, wraps a towel around his waist, and washes the feet of the disciples. Footwashing was traditionally offered to guests as an act of hospitality upon their visit to one's home. Traditionally, a servant would offer it as an act of service. So when Jesus rises from the table to wash the disciples' feet, they are rightly shocked. Peter declares, "You will never wash my feet" (13:8). Jesus responds, "Unless I wash you have no share with me" (13:8). So Peter says, "Lord, not my feet but also my hands and head!" (13:9). Returning to his seat, Jesus expounds upon the action he has shared with them: "If I, your Lord and teacher, have washed your feet, you ought to wash one another's feet" (13:14). This story is often used to promote mission and service, and that is certainly an element of the lesson. But the main thrust of this teaching (not surprisingly, considering it is one of the main themes of the gospel) is invitation: "I tell you now, before it occurs, so that when it does occur you may believe that I AM" (13:19).

Throughout John we have read references to Jesus's death and resurrection long before they occur— sometimes years before. Basically, John says, Jesus's disciples didn't get the message at this time, but following his resurrection, they remembered and believed. Jesus is laying that foundation here. He is planting a seed for their post-resurrection memory to recall. Believe what? What are the disciples missing now—so near the end? The disciples are wondering who Jesus is; how can the Messiah wash feet like a common servant and go on and on about being lifted up? Jesus still invites and encourages. He called them to be his disciples many chapters and years ago, but he still knows their hearts. They need the words of invitation now and in the days to come more than ever.

Jesus uses footwashing as a metaphor for the service the disciples ought to offer to each other and the world. But it is more than an act of loving-kindness. It is a reflection of a relationship and fellowship the believer has with Jesus Christ. The disciples and Jesus share a unique intimacy with one another. Following the footwashing, Jesus tells the disciples that one of them will soon betray him. We learn that the betrayer is Judas, who is instructed by Jesus to "Do quickly what you are going to do" (13:27). Judas leaves the scene, and the narrator says, "And it was night" (13:30).

The use of the word "night" throughout John is significant. One of the "I am" sayings of Jesus is "I AM the Light of the World." Nicodemus comes to Jesus by night. The soldiers Judas will soon bring to arrest Jesus in the garden carry lanterns and torches. This is not just to indicate the time of day but to emphasis the darkness of their spiritual understanding. Before Mary encounters the risen Christ at the tomb, we are told it was still dark. So it is not a coincidence that Judas leaves the table and steps into darkness: "And it was night." What does it look like to experience darkness? What does "and it was night" add to the story?

For the Preacher and Teacher

Why is it significant that this meal is *before* Passover? What is lost or gained by a different understanding of this meal with the disciples? What do we learn about the character of Jesus and the disciples from this shared meal? How do the teachings around this table echo the mission of the church? How do you understand the reaction of the disciples to Jesus washing their feet? How would you react? Have you ever participated in a footwashing service? What was your reaction? What does the act of footwashing tell us about the relationship between Jesus and the disciples? What is at the heart of his command that they should wash others' feet?

The Beloved Disciple (13:23)

Only John offers the perspective of an anonymous disciple throughout the passion story. Many participants in Bible studies over the years have referred to this disciple simply as "John," the author of the gospel, and some consider him to be the apostle John, the brother of James. I disagree with the latter opinion and would amend the former. I believe there is more to this stranger than a self-portrait of the writer; he is a symbol of the community that produced the gospel.

When I was a kid, I often watched the *Speed Racer* cartoon. I imagined one day I would own my own Mach 5. One of the more mysterious characters on the show was Racer X, a guy who drove a yellow and black car and wore a mask. No one knew his name, so he was simply Racer X. Turns out he was Speed's brother, presumed dead. He would show up at just the right moment to save Speed or fight off the bad guys so that Speed would win the race. The anonymous disciple in John reminds me of Racer X, so I often refer to him as "Disciple X." He only shows up at a few places, but when he does, we learn new perspectives and lessons. Here, at the table, this disciple (we'll refer to him as John, but keep in mind, we are thinking more in terms of an early Christian community than an individual) reclines at the heart of Jesus. This position is symbolic of the Gospel of John's relationship to Jesus. It is one of intimacy more than privilege and recalls the language of 1:18, which describes the relationship of Jesus to God the Father: "Close to the Father's heart, who has made him known." Now it is John, or the community of early believers in Jesus, who is "making [God] known" to us. Just as Jesus shared a unique relationship to the Father, so this community understood its relationship to Jesus to be unique. This relationship gives the gospel a sense of authenticity. Sitting at the table—next to the very heart of Jesus—is a great honor.

When Jesus announces that one of the disciples will betray him, their responses are different here than in the Synoptic Gospels. They do not go around the table, asking, "Lord, is it I?" Peter turns to Disciple X to find the answers, and the disciple asks the question of Jesus. The response is, "It is the one to whom I give this piece of bread" (13:26). Jesus gives the bread to Judas, who promptly leaves. But everyone else around the table received the bread too. None of the disciples names Judas as the betrayer at this point; they all receive bread from Jesus. John is quick to identify Satan as the one who compels Judas to act.

Jumping ahead, we find the beloved disciple again in John 18:15. He accompanies Peter throughout Jesus's trial by the religious authorities. Disciple X, we are told, was known by the high priest, and so he gains access for Peter to enter the courtyard. We encounter the beloved disciple again at the cross, standing with Jesus's mother. Speaking to Mary and John, Jesus says, "Behold your son" and "Behold your mother," and the gospel writer adds the footnote, "And from that moment on [Disciple X] took [Mary] into his home" (John 19:26, 27). So a new community is created even as one ends. Jesus dies on the cross, but his last act is to create a home for both his mother and his disciple. They are to care for one another so that neither faces the world alone. But there is more to the story than two people looking after each other. Jesus creates a new community, one the church is meant to model to the world. This community is defined by its love for Jesus, his love for them, and a radical sharing of this love with the world. The church is meant to share this relationship with those within and outside its community. The unique relationship of Jesus to Disciple X is meant to be reflected in how the church is related to the world.

Later, we see Disciple X in the garden on the day of resurrection (20:1–10). In chapter 21, the disciples go fishing, and it is Disciple X—not Peter—who is the first to recognize Jesus: "It is the Lord!" (21:7). It's an early affirmation of faith. This is one of the most important functions of the church: to see, know, and proclaim the presence of God in our midst. At the end of chapter 21, the writer identifies himself with Disciple X, but more important is the idea that this disciple will never die. That is, as long as the church maintains its intimate relationship to Jesus and the world, it will exist forever.

For the Preacher and Teacher

What does the beloved disciple add or detract from the passion narrative? Is it helpful to think of this disciple as more of a symbol than a specific person? What do we learn about John's community through the eyes and actions of this anonymous disciple? And what does he have to say about the relationship of the church to the world?

Prayers for the Disciples (John 14–17)

These four chapters are unique to John, although some of the teachings are echoed elsewhere. What is distinctive about John's account is the context: basically, these are four chapters of intercessory prayers by Jesus for the disciples. At the end of chapter 14, they leave the room where they had dinner together and walk to the garden where Jesus will be arrested. Jesus is fully aware of the events that will soon take place and of the disciples' confusion and remorse. Selections from chapter 14 of John are often read at funerals; they are words of hope and promise in the midst of pain and grief. A great way to explore these chapters is to experience them rather than study them. Over the years of Bible study, I have simply read these chapters aloud to Bible study groups in the days of Holy Week, just before Jesus's arrest and crucifixion are commemorated in worship. It is a very powerful experience.

For the Preacher and Teacher

What do Jesus's words convey about his relationship to the disciples? If you have a chance to hear them read aloud or you can read them aloud to a group, consider these questions: What emotions do you hear from Jesus? What difference does hearing, rather than studying, these words make? How do these words add to the relationship with the disciples we first explored with regard to footwashing? In your own life, what would Jesus pray for?

Betrayal and Arrest (John 18)

In John 18, the scene shifts to the Kidron Valley, "where there was a garden" (18:1). The other gospels refer to this place as Gethsemane, but the term "garden of Gethsemane," as it is often referred to, does not exist in Scripture. In John's garden, Jesus acts radically different than the way he is portrayed in the Synoptics. He does not ask Peter, James, and John to pray with him. The disciples do not struggle to remain awake. Jesus sees Judas coming with a detachment of temple police carrying lanterns and torches. This detail is omitted in the other versions, but it fits in John's overall theology. Jesus has already identified himself as the Light of the World. The soldiers' lanterns and torches reveal their own spiritual darkness. They too, like Judas, are in the dark. There is no betrayer's kiss, no sweating blood, no comforting angels. Jesus is in complete control of the entire scene when he asks, "Whom are you looking for?" (18:4). Interestingly, this is the question Jesus asked his prospective disciples in chapter 1. "Jesus of Nazareth," the soldiers respond. "I am he," Jesus says in our English translations (18:5). But by now, you know what he says in the Greek text:

"I AM" (18:5). Remember: this is the name of God. Upon hearing God's name invoked, the powerful soldiers fall to the ground. Jesus stands over them and repeats the same question: "Whom are you looking for?" They answer in likewise the same way. "I told you that I AM. So if you are looking for me let these men go" (18:8). Peter cuts off the ear of Malchus, but Jesus chastises him by saying, "Put your sword back in its sheath. Am I not to drink of the cup that the Father has given me?" (18:11). Jesus not only accepts these events, but he is an active participant in them.

For the Preacher and Teacher

Does John's portrayal of Jesus reflect what you know, or is it unfamiliar? How does Jesus act differently here than the others? What does all this say about John's understanding of theology?

The Trial of Jesus

First, Jesus is brought before Annas and then Caiphas, the high priest. Unlike the other accounts of when Jesus is questioned, he does not remain silent. The same thing happens when Jesus is brought before the Roman governor, Pontius Pilate: he is not silent. An interesting detail, found only in John, concerns the praetorium, Pilate's headquarters. The Jewish leaders will not enter it so as not to defile themselves for the Passover (remember: Passover has not yet happened, unlike in the Synoptics). They are more concerned about following the religious rules than accusing an innocent man of treason and blasphemy. So Pilate has to go outside to speak to the Jewish leaders and then back inside to speak to Jesus. This folly happens over and over again until Pilate finally brings Jesus outside toward the end of chapter 18. When Pilate questions Jesus, his words are phrased just that way in the English translations—as questions. But in the Greek text, these are *statements*. Pilate, in the English translations, asks, "Are you the King of the Jews?" (18:33). The Greek text says, "You are the King of the Jews."

This is not a small detail. Maybe Pilate is being sarcastic by referring to this prisoner as a king. Still, he is betrayed by his own words. Ironically, Pilate speaks—testifies beyond his current level of knowledge—to the truth. This brings us to another of Jesus's "I am" sayings: "I AM the way, the truth and the life. No one comes to the Father except through me" (John 14:6). This verse is often quoted out of context to either invalidate other non-Christian religious traditions or to pose a threat:

affirm Christ as Lord and Savior or leave yourself open to the consequences. Of course, neither of these ideas has any home in the Gospel of John. Remember that Jesus's primary mission is to *invite* people, not turn them away. Jesus's invitation even extends to Pilate—the one who has authority to execute Jesus—who says, "Everyone who belongs to the truth listens to my voice" (18:37). Pilate responds, "What is truth?" (18:38). Jesus does not respond, and it doesn't matter because we know that he is the way, the truth, and the life.

For the Preacher and Teacher

What do you make of Pontius Pilate? Do a quick search about him to add some historical context to his interaction with Jesus. What motivates him? What is at risk for Pilate—professionally and personally? How is he depicted differently between the various gospel accounts? What is Jesus inviting Pilate to do or be?

Jesus and Barabbas (John 18:33–40)

All four gospels tell us about Pilate's custom of releasing a prisoner at Passover. There are several questions about this practice, not the least of which is why would a Roman governor—charged with keeping the peace in one of the most hostile corners of the Empire—offer to release Barabbas, of all people? Barabbas is a known terrorist, insurrectionist, and murderer; he is basically the last person Pilate would release. It is clear from the four accounts that Pilate believed Jesus to be innocent and wanted him to be released. Now maybe Pilate was a shrewd gambler and knew the people would prefer to release the innocent Jesus over the violent Barabbas. One would think Pilate would offer to release a prisoner being held for a mere misdemeanor (like traffic tickets or jaywalking). But Pilate offers to release the kind of troublemaker he most feared.

Here's the issue: the tradition of Pilate releasing a criminal at Passover can be found nowhere outside the gospel accounts. We have several non-Christian historians recording events during Pilate's rule. He was not a popular guy with anyone, so the stories are not flattering. Yet none of those accounts ever mentions anything about releasing a criminal at Passover. The gospel writers are making a theological rather than an historical point. The name Barabbas means "son of the father" in Aramaic, the form of Hebrew spoken during Jesus's lifetime. Pilate unknowingly and ironically offers to release the one called *son of the father* or the one who is the actual Son of the Father. But the crowds choose Barabbas.

Their choice betrays their own complicity—and ours too—in Jesus's death. As much as Peter and Judas, we deny Jesus.

For the Preacher and Teacher

Why is it significant that the tradition of releasing a prisoner at Passover appears only in the gospels? What meaning do you find in the translation of Barabbas's name? How do we deny Christ today? How easy or difficult is it to acknowledge our complicity in his death? And what commentary does John offer about our choice of Barabbas over Jesus? What does it say about humanity?

The Death of the Messiah (John 19:1–37)

Jesus's long-awaited "hour" has come—his crucifixion. Unlike the other gospel accounts, no one shouts at Jesus in John. The criminals crucified with him do not deride him, and he does not languish and shout in pain. Only in John does a scene of profound love occur at the foot of the cross. We see two people who believed in Jesus: his mother, Mary, and one of his disciples. The two hold each other on a day of great pain and grief. Looking down at them, Jesus remembers each—the memories, the stories, the lives they shared together.

The only reference we find to Mary, aside from being present at Jesus's crucifixion, is at the wedding of Cana in Galilee (John 2), where she says to the steward, "Do whatever he tells you" (2:5). In this comment, I detect a couple of messages. The first is pride. This is my boy. He'll take care of this. The second is faith. Jesus has power and ability and can make any situation right. Standing at the foot of the cross, his mother remembers these and other stories about her son. We share her grief. But she experiences more than just loss; she sees in his eyes the very heart of God.

The church teaches that Mary was Jesus's first disciple. From the moment of his conception, Mary shared in his life—not only as a mother but as a faithful, committed follower. She did not abandon him at the end. Those condemned to crucifixion were not hung twenty feet in the air or so, as is often portrayed in art. It was more like seven feet above ground. So Mary is not quite eye level—more like waist level—and she is able to clearly hear Jesus's words from the cross, referring to the disciple standing with her. He asks, "Woman, here is your son" (19:26).

Who is this disciple? It's Disciple X again, last seen helping Peter gain access to the courtyard outside the building where Jesus was being tried by the religious leaders (18:15). This disciple and Jesus enjoyed an intimacy that Jesus shared with no one else. He learns that Jesus is faithful to his promise. Just the day before, Jesus said to all the disciples, "I will not leave you orphaned" (14:18). While the other disciples are absent from the cross, this man is right there, accepting the responsibility for caring for Jesus's mother: "Here is your mother" (19:27).

By linking these two together, "Behold your son/ Behold your mother," Jesus creates a bond of intimacy, trust, and mutual affection. The only thing these two people share in common is their love for and their belief in Jesus. He is their Lord, their Christ, and their Savior. Their faith is obvious to us because they are present to the end. Their relationship to each other—and to Jesus—marks the very best definition we have for church. It is a community of like-minded folk who love and care for one another as a result of their relationships to each other and the one they affirm as Lord and Savior.

For the Preacher and Teacher

There is more at play here than Jesus finding a common home for his mother and friend. What significance does this interchange at the cross have for us? What do we learn about the character of Jesus? The relationship between Mary and Disciple X is characterized by their love for Jesus. The same can be said for the church. We should live out our love in faith and obedience: "By this everyone will know you are my disciples, if you have love for one another" (13:35). How do we do that?

The Resurrection of the Messiah (20:1–29)

The Gospel of John devotes a significant amount of time to Mary Magdalene on Easter morning. She arrives before dawn "while it was still dark" (20:1). We've seen this use of "dark" before; it is a diagnosis of Mary's spiritual condition, the darkness of her grief. After finding the tomb open and empty, Mary runs to Peter and Disciple X; they return with her to the garden to examine things. They then return to the house; only Mary lingers. She encounters two angels who ask her why she is weeping. Then Jesus appears, although Mary does not recognize him. He asks, "Why are you weeping? Whom are you looking for?" (20:15). Jesus has asked this second question before of prospective disciples (1:38); he also asks it of the guards who come to Gethsemane to arrest him before his trial (18: 4, 7). As always in John, Jesus is inviting with his words. Upon hearing Jesus speak her name, Mary recognizes Jesus. Remember one of his "I am" sayings: "I am the Good Shepherd ... He calls his own sheep by name and leads them out. I know my own and my own know me" (10:3, 14).

For the Preacher and Teacher

Why does Mary fail to recognize Jesus? What is she missing that Jesus offers her so that she can see him? What barriers do emotions like grief present to us?

Jesus, the Disciples, and Thomas (John 20:19–29)

Again, we see more of the same character of Jesus throughout John; he initiates contact with others. He invites them to change their confusion and doubt into joy. Somehow, he enters the house where the disciples are secretly gathered and offers to show them his hands and side. Thomas was not present at the initial meeting, so he is doubtful when the disciples say to him, "We have seen the Lord!" (These are the same words Mary Magdalene used following her encounter with the risen Lord in 20:18). It is plausible that the other disciples had a similar reaction to Mary's testimony earlier about seeing the risen Lord. Thomas will not believe until he sees and touches Jesus's wounds. So Jesus shows up and offers exactly that. He says to Thomas, "Put your finger here and see my hands. Reach out your hand and put it in my side. Do not doubt but believe" (20:27).

For the Teacher and Preacher

Is it fair to label Thomas "doubting" if he was absent when Jesus first appeared? Jesus knew he needed physical proof to believe such an incredible story. Jesus knew Mary only needed to hear her name spoken. If the risen Christ appeared to you, what would he offer you to aid in your understanding?

A Sermon

Why include an All Saints Day sermon in a section devoted to Jesus's passion and resurrection? As the sermon explains the origins of the observance, it is explicitly linked to Christianity's most holy day.

"From All Saints to Easter: From Death to Life"
John 11:32–44
A Sermon for All Saints Day
November 1, 2015
Custer Road United Methodist Church,
Lectio Teaching Worship Service

The four of them were very good friends. Jesus spent many hours in Bethany at the home of Martha, Mary, and Lazarus. They shared food and stories together. The bonds they shared were unique for all four. Mary, Martha, and Lazarus were companions of Jesus, but they were also followers and students. Jesus shared familial relationships with each of them but also accepted their faith in him as Lord and Savior. So it must have been very troubling when Jesus received word that Lazarus, referred to only as "the one you love" in the sisters' note, was gravely ill. They waited for Jesus to return to Judea with growing impatience and worry. After two days and no response from Jesus, Lazarus died. The grief was overwhelming. But Martha and Mary felt more than the loss of a loved one; they also resented Jesus for ignoring their plea for help.

So when Jesus showed up four days after Lazarus' death, it was more than the sisters could take. They were already burdened by the funeral preparations, expenses, and the constant visitors. They required a steady energy to entertain others while, at the same time, feeling exhausted by their own pain. When Martha heard that Jesus was in town, she left Mary at home to deal with the guests and took off. Finding him on the road, she lamented, "Lord, if you had been here my brother wouldn't have died." *My brother.* Not the one Jesus loved, as the note had said a few days earlier. Martha added, "But even now I know that whatever you ask God, God will give you." Hope. She had seen Jesus do amazing things. Everyone knew of his power over life and death. Jesus confirmed her hope, saying, "Your brother will rise again." *Your brother.* "I know he will rise in the resurrection on the last day." "I am the resurrection and the life. Whoever believes in me will live, even though they die. Everyone who lives and believes in me will never die. Do you believe this?"

Do you believe this?

Martha professes faith in God's ability to work through Jesus by stating, "I know God will give whatever you ask." Now she affirms her faith in Jesus himself: "Yes, Lord, I believe that you are the Christ, God's Son, the one who is coming into the world."

Today is All Saints Day, the day the church set aside 1500 years ago to commemorate and remember the lives of those who have died in faith. Originally, Christians remembered the names of every person martyred for faith in Christ. Every Sunday of the year contained some remembrance of a fallen brother or sister in Christ. But that list became too big too fast, so efforts were made to remember large numbers of Christians on a single day.

The first known occurrence for a day of Christian remembrance for the lives of the faithful was called by Saint Basil in the year 397, in Caesarea. Pope Boniface IV inaugurated a church-wide day of remembrance on May 13, 609, in Rome. On that day, the ancient Parthenon (a former pagan temple) was consecrated a church, and the feast day of Mary and the martyrs was proclaimed. May thirteenth had been a traditional pagan day of remembrance for departed spirits, but it was now co-opted by the church as a Christian observance during the season of Easter. A century later, Pope Gregory III (731–741 CE) severed the link to the ancient pagan commemoration by permanently moving All Saints Day to November first. In modern practice, on All Saints Day we remember the lives of individuals who helped to form our faith, as well as members of the church who died over the previous twelve months. We will read those names in a few moments.

One of the most unique and important elements of the Christian faith is that we believe God's power and ability to save is even stronger than death. Through our faith in the resurrection of Jesus, we—along with every faithful believer—will also be raised from death. All Saints Day is not just another date on the calendar. It is a day to affirm what we believe. Unlike other faiths, we do not believe that life is an endless pursuit of karma, where we return to earth over and over again in different forms until we get everything right. We do not believe in the pursuit of nirvana, a state of blessedness in balance with the universe. Remembering that All Saints was originally included in the season of Easter, on this day, we affirm that the end of human life is only the beginning of everlasting life with God. We allow God to transform our grief into hope, death into life, darkness into light. We affirmed our faith earlier by reading the words of the Nicene Creed: "We look for the resurrection of the dead, and the life of the world to come."

The other lectionary readings for today speak of visions of salvation God shared with prophets, who then shared them with us:

> On this mountain, the Lord of heavenly forces will prepare for all peoples a rich feast, a feast of choice wines, of select foods rich in flavor, of choice wines well refined. He will swallow up on this mountain the veil that is veiling all peoples, the shroud enshrouding all nations. He will swallow up death forever, The Lord God will wipe away tears from every face; he will remove his people's disgrace from off the whole earth, for the Lord has spoken. They will say on that day, "Look! This is our God, for whom we have waited—and he has saved us! This is the Lord for whom we have waited; let's be glad and rejoice in his salvation!" (Isaiah 25:6–9)

> Then I saw a new heaven and a new earth, for the former heaven and the former earth had passed away, and the

sea was no more. I saw the holy city,
New Jerusalem, coming down out of
heaven from God, made ready as a bride
dressed beautifully for her husband.
I heard a loud voice from the thrown
say, "Look! God's dwelling is here with
humankind. He will dwell with them,
and they will be his peoples. God himself
will be with them as their God. He will
wipe away every tear from their eyes.
Death will be no more. There will be no
mourning, crying, or pain any more, for
the former things have passed away."
Then the one seated on the throne said,
"Look! I have made all things new." He
also said, "Write these things down, for
these words are trustworthy and true."
Then he said to me, "All is done. I am the
Alpha and the Omega, the beginning
and the end." (Revelation 21:1–6a)

These prophetic visions remind us that life has
a purpose, and God calls us into a future where
death and fear are replaced with joy and celebration.
Isaiah's feast on the mountain for all people is
recalled in our liturgy for Holy Communion, where we
anticipate feasting at Christ's heavenly banquet. The
book of Revelation's vision of a new heaven, earth,

city, and dwelling place for God among humanity is often read at funerals, expressing confidence in God's ability to wipe away our tears forever.

After speaking with Jesus, Martha returned home and told Mary that Jesus was looking for her. Mary found Jesus on the road and greeted him with the same words her sister had used: "Lord, if you had been here my brother would not have died." Jesus expressed his own grief and loss over the death of Lazarus, feeling "greatly disturbed" in spirit and shedding tears. Arriving at the tomb, Jesus ordered the stone to be removed. Martha, not at home any longer but joining the scene at the tomb, protested, "No Lord. The stench will be too strong." Four days had not been enough time to deaden the acuteness of her grief. "Didn't I tell you that if you believed you would see God's glory?" Jesus asked, and his frustration with Martha's grief was obvious in his words. At Jesus's command, Lazarus, "the dead man," walked out of the tomb—his hands, feet, and head still wrapped in the burial cloths. Jesus said, "Unbind him, and let him go."

As we remember our saints this morning, the power of grief may still be a binding around us. Their lives touched our own in very profound ways, and the sadness of the months or years since their deaths may still pierce us. To commemorate the names of our loved ones on All Saints Day is not to deny the reality of grief or to shame the loss we feel. We simply affirm what our faith teaches us about life and death, that Jesus's words to Martha on the road to Bethany are as true to us as they were to her: "I am the resurrection and the life. Whoever believes in me will live, even if they die. Everyone who lives and believes in me will never die. Do you believe this?"

Do you believe this?

May we set aside the funeral clothes of mourning and brokenness and celebrate the victory our faithful saints have achieved over the power of death. May we walk into newness of life today, as Lazarus walked away from his tomb and as Jesus later stepped out of his own tomb. May we live into God's visions of a future without pain or suffering, one even without death, where we will feast at the Lord's everlasting table in the presence of our loved ones who lived, died, and were resurrected in the Christian faith.

Yes, Lord, we believe you are the Christ, God's Son—the one who is coming into the world!

In the name of the Father, the Son, and the Holy Spirit, amen.

Epilogue and Invitation

John 20:30–31

While it is true that John includes a chapter 21, most scholars believe it was added later. The resurrection appearance there is very similar to those we read in the Synoptics. The end of chapter 20, however, is unique for several reasons:

1. It reads like an ending. "These words are written ..." (20:31) sounds like a final message to the reader.
2. The words "believe" and "believing," central to John's theology, both appear in this account, so it is consistent with the rest of the gospel.
3. The strong invitational nature of the ending continues the message we have heard from the beginning of the gospel. This language is absent from chapter 21.

None of this means that chapter 21 is not worth reading; it contains wonderful lessons of redemption and the mission of the church.

Following Jesus's death and resurrection, the Gospel of John says, "Now Jesus did many other signs in the presence of his disciples, which are not written in this book. But these are written so that you may come to believe that Jesus is the Messiah, the Son of God, and that through believing you may have life in his name" (20:30–31). We are invited to accept Jesus's great love for us and become his disciples. From his cross, looking upon each of us with the same love and compassion he had for Mary and the disciple—a love you and I could never imagine or understand—Jesus asks each of us, "Do you believe this?"

If you have not known this love before, may you receive it right now. Jesus said, "No one has greater love than this, to lay down one's life for one's friends" (15:13). You are Jesus's friend. He loves you—all of you. That love includes your brokenness, your imperfections, and your mistakes. Acknowledge Jesus's lordship of your life, and walk in the abundant life he promises for all who love him.

If you have already accepted Christ's love for you and count yourself as his disciple, then live out your love in faith and obedience. Remember that he said, "By this everyone will know you are my disciples, if you have love for one another" (13:35).

Several years ago, I presided at a funeral. I do not remember today whose funeral it was—maybe a parishioner or extended family of a church member. What I remember was a comment shared with me following the burial at the cemetery. A young man approached me, shook my hand, and said, "I could tell you really believed what you said." This was not the usual, "nice service," or "good job" preachers normally hear after a funeral. I was sort of taken aback. My response was pretty strange: "Well, yeah." Not the most pastoral response ever. But my immediate reaction was, "Of course I believe this stuff. I am a Christian. I am a pastor. This is what I do. Well, yeah."

If I had a time machine, there are many places in the past I would want to visit. One is that cemetery in Duncanville a decade or so ago. When the guy says, "I can tell you really believe this," I would have a more thoughtful, articulate response—more than "Well, yeah." In Jesus's love, there is a longing, a community, and an authentic relationship that gives our lives meaning. "Yes, Lord, we believe!" St. Augustine said, "You have made us restless, O Lord, and our hearts are restless until they find rest in you." May our restless hearts find their rest in the love of Jesus Christ!

CPSIA information can be obtained at www.ICGtesting.com
Printed in the USA
BVOW02*2050010616

450347BV00013B/392/P